959.704
FER
C.1
2002
18.95

DATE DUE

American Symbols
AND THEIR Meanings

THE
VIETNAM
VETERANS
MEMORIAL

American Symbols AND THEIR Meanings

The Vietnam Veterans Memorial

Joseph Ferry

Mason Crest Publishers
Philadelphia

18.95
2002

First printing

1 3 5 7 9 8 6 4 2

Library of Congress Cataloging-in-Publication Data
on file at the Library of Congress

ISBN 1-59084-039-9

Publisher's note: all quotations in this book come
from original sources, and contain the spelling and
grammatical inconsistencies of the original text.

American Symbols
AND THEIR **Meanings**

CONTENTS

Introduction

THE IMPORTANCE OF AMERICAN SYMBOLS

Symbols are not merely ornaments to admire—they also tell us stories. If you look at one of them closely, you may want to find out why it was made and what it truly means. If you ask people who live in the society in which the symbol exists, you will learn some things. But by studying the people who created that symbol and the reasons why they made it, you will understand the deepest meanings of that symbol.

The United States owes its identity to great events in history, and the most remarkable American Symbols are rooted in these events. The struggle for independence from Great Britain gave America the Declaration of Independence, the Liberty Bell, the American flag, and other images of freedom. The War of 1812 gave the young country a song dedicated to the flag, "The Star-Spangled Banner," which became our national anthem. Nature gave the country its national animal, the bald eagle. These symbols established the identity of the new nation, and set it apart from the nations of the Old World.

To be emotionally moving, a symbol must strike people with a sense of power and unity. But it often takes a long time for a new symbol to be accepted by all the people, especially if there are older symbols that have gradually lost popularity. For example, the image of Uncle Sam has replaced Brother Jonathan, an earlier representation of the national will, while the Statue of Liberty has replaced Columbia, a woman who represented liberty to Americans in the early 19th century. Since then, Uncle Sam and the Statue of Liberty have endured and have become cherished icons of America.

Of all the symbols, the Statue of Liberty has perhaps the most curious story, for unlike other symbols, Americans did not create her. She was created by the French, who then gave her to America. Hence, she represented not what Americans thought of their country but rather what the French thought of America. It was many years before Americans decided to accept this French goddess of Liberty as a symbol for the United States and its special role among the nations: to spread freedom and enlighten the world.

This series of books is valuable because it presents the story of each of America's great symbols in a freshly written way and will contribute to the students' knowledge and awareness of them. It is to be hoped that this information will awaken an abiding interest in American history, as well as in the meanings of American symbols.

—Barry Moreno,
librarian and historian
Ellis Island/Statue of Liberty National Monument

The reflection of these flowers can be seen in the black granite of the Vietnam Veterans Memorial. Carved into the long black wall are the names of every soldier who died in the Vietnam War. The wall is the most popular memorial in Washington, D.C. with more than 4.4 million visitors each year.

THE WALL THAT HEALS

*I*t is a warm spring afternoon in Washington D.C. Thousands of visitors have come to the National Mall to soak up history and explore the sights of the city.

A few people linger at the Lincoln Memorial, built in honor of the president who fought for equality among all men. Others stop to remember the contributions made by Thomas Jefferson at a memorial built in his honor. Still others gaze at the imposing Washington Monument.

By far, however, most people stop by the Vietnam Veterans Memorial, a long, black wall sunk down in the earth, tucked away in a corner of the Mall.

A man approaches slowly, almost hesitating as he comes closer. He gazes at the impressive wall, and then hangs his head silently. A few minutes later, he approaches the shiny wall, *etched* with the names of more than 58,200 men killed during the Vietnam War. His eyes search the rows and columns. Finally, he finds the name of a friend who died in the war.

The man reaches out toward the wall, his *weathered* hands trembling. His fingers gently trace the letters of his friend's name.

The man begins to cry.

It is an emotional scene repeated thousands of times each year. The Vietnam Veterans Memorial is a powerful symbol of American freedom because of all that it repre-sents: the bloody struggle against a shadowy foe 10,000 miles from American soil and the intense reaction at home from people who had a hard time understanding what the war was all about.

When the Vietnam Veterans Memorial was dedicated in 1982, many veterans experienced mixed emotions. Although they had returned from the war years before, often the greeting awaiting them was anything but welcoming. The memorial was meant as a way to recognize and honor these veterans for their many sacrifices.

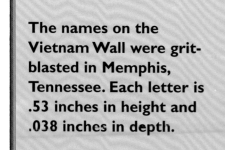

The names on the Vietnam Wall were grit-blasted in Memphis, Tennessee. Each letter is .53 inches in height and .038 inches in depth.

Many people hoped the memorial would be a place where veterans could find closure. It was nicknamed, "the wall that heals." Having a memorial built, in many cases, allowed veterans to reflect, to remember lost friends, and to heal psychological wounds.

While the memorial originally was meant to honor those who served in the military, it has come to have a profound impact on even those with no connection to the Vietnam War. Few visitors to the memorial are left untouched by the *symbolism* of the memorial. The thousands of international visitors may know little about the Vietnam War and the United States' involvement in that conflict, but often they too are awestruck by the memorial.

Young people also visit the Vietnam Veterans Memorial. The connection for them varies, much as it does for adults. Many young people come to see the name of a relative—perhaps a father, mother, or grandparent. These children have grown up recognizing the relevance of the memorial because the Vietnam War impacted some member of their family. For these children the role of the memorial is obvious. However, most children who visit do not possess such a personal connection. In the minds of many young people, the Vietnam War is ancient history.

An American napalm bomb explodes in a field outside Saigon during the Vietnam War. Napalm was used against Vietnamese troops during the war; it kills by suffocating and burning its victims. The Vietnam War was a brutal conflict that took a terrible toll on both the Vietnamese people and on the young American soldiers forced to fight in the war.

THE VIETNAM WAR

he roots of the war in Vietnam go back to the late 1940s, just after the end of World War II. For many years, the French had ruled Vietnam, a small country in Southeast Asia. But the Vietnamese people wanted to rule themselves. Led by a man named Ho Chi Minh, they began a fight for freedom, not unlike the U.S. war against Britain almost 200 years earlier.

It took nine years, but the Vietnamese people won their war for independence. Although the French gave up their claim to rule the country, it did not mean the end of problems for the Vietnamese people.

Ho Chi Minh and his followers wanted a government

like the Soviet Union and China had at the time. But some citizens did not want such an *oppressive* government. At a special peace meeting in 1954, an agreement was reached to split Vietnam into two parts, with two separate governments. North Vietnam had a Communist government headed by Ho Chi Minh. South Vietnam had a government led by Ngo Dinh Diem, who had spent his whole life fighting against *Communism*.

Eventually, the two parts of the country were to be

When fighting broke out in Vietnam, the United States supported the government of South Vietnam, which was controlled by Ngo Dinh Diem (seated, top). It was U.S. policy to oppose the spread of communism. The leader of the North Vietnamese government, Ho Chi Minh (right), was a communist.

joined together following an election to decide whether the government of the North or the government of the South would rule all of Vietnam. But the leaders of South Vietnam refused to participate in the elections. They felt that the Communist government of North Vietnam would not permit fair elections.

It didn't take long for trouble to begin. Many people in South Vietnam did not like Diem's government because they felt it was dishonest and unfair. They favored Ho Chi Minh's rule.

By the late 1950s, a group of *rebels* known as Viet Cong began to fight against their own military forces in South Vietnam. Sensing an opportunity to control the entire country, the government of North Vietnam began to supply the rebels with weapons and soldiers.

Soon, there was an all-out war.

The United States decided to help Diem, even though his government was *corrupt* and many of his own people did not like him. One of the reasons U.S. leaders wanted to help Diem was because they did not want Communism to spread through Southeast Asia. If Communists ruled Southeast Asia, U.S. leaders were afraid the whole world could eventually fall.

At first, the U.S. sent only war supplies and a few hundred soldiers. These troops were supposed to teach the South Vietnamese military how to fight. Most Americans at the time had only a vague knowledge of what was going on halfway around the world.

But as the years passed, South Vietnam needed more and more help, so the United States started sending more money and more men. With no end to the war in sight, the U.S. stepped up its involvement in 1965 by sending troops to fight side-by-side with the South Vietnamese military.

At first, only a few thousand American soldiers were sent to Vietnam. But as the months passed, thousands more arrived. By 1967, more than 500,000 Americans were fighting the war in Vietnam.

Because of television, Vietnam was the first war that Americans could watch in their living rooms. Every night, people watched the news to see nightmarish scenes from the daily battles. They saw houses burning and wounded and bloody American soldiers. They saw dead women and children sprawled in the mud.

At home, Americans began to take sides on the war. Some believed the United States government had a responsibility to stop the spread of Communism. They supported the war effort and were known as "hawks." But others, mostly college students, felt the United States had no business being in the war. They were known as "doves" and favored letting the Vietnamese people work out their own problems.

As the war dragged on, there were more protests in the United States. The biggest peace march in history took place in Washington, D.C., in 1969, when more than 250,000 protested America's part in the Vietnam War.

A U.S. Marine carries an elderly Vietnamese woman to a helicopter. The woman and her family were being evacuated from a combat zone in March 1970. They were taken to a refugee center.

In 1973, 14 years after the first American had died in Vietnam, the U.S. forces began to pull out of Vietnam. A peace treaty between the U.S. and the government of North Vietnam brought the fighting to an end. The last Americans left Vietnam in 1975, just as the army of North Vietnam took control of South Vietnam.

Almost 60,000 Americans died in the war and more than 300,000 had been wounded. Yet the U.S. government did not achieve its goal of stopping Communists from taking control of South Vietnam, a fact that caused many veterans to wonder why they had been forced to fight in the first place.

Vietnam veterans sit in front of an upside-down American flag—a distress symbol—during a protest against the war in 1969. Many people were unhappy about the Vietnam War; unfortunately, because of this the soldiers often did not receive a warm welcome home. Many veterans felt bitter that their country, which they had served, seemed to ignore them.

THE IDEA FOR A MEMORIAL

A memorial in honor of Vietnam veterans was the brainchild of Jan Scruggs, one of more than 2.7 million Americans to fight in the war. A decorated *infantryman* and winner of the Purple Heart, Scruggs was one of the lucky ones who made it home from the jungles of Southeast Asia in one piece.

In 1979, 10 years after his tour of duty in Vietnam, Scruggs and his wife saw a movie about the war called *The Deer Hunter*. Scenes from the movie made him remember the dangerous days and nights in the hot, steamy Vietnam jungle. He once said of his service in Vietnam, "The bitterness I feel when I remember carrying the lifeless bodies of close friends through the mire of Vietnam will probably never *subside*. I still wonder if anything can be found to bring any purpose to all the suffering and death."

Scruggs struggled for a year in Vietnam to escape the clutches of death. He now found himself committed to a different struggle, this one to enshrine the memory of those who fought so bravely and died in Vietnam.

In late 1979, Scruggs met with a group of Vietnam veterans in Washington, D.C. He expressed his belief that ordinary American citizens would donate money to build a memorial to those who fought and died in Vietnam. Some veterans thought it foolish to hold such a belief. Still, Scruggs would persevere.

Scruggs and a group of fellow veterans formed the Vietnam Veterans Memorial Fund (VVMF). The objective of the group was to create a *tangible* tribute to those Americans who served in the Vietnam War in the form of the Vietnam Veterans Memorial.

When word got out that a group of Vietnam veterans were intent on building a memorial to veterans of the Vietnam War through public donations, members of the newly formed VVMF found themselves *scrutinized* and ridiculed. On the CBS *Evening News* one night, correspondent Roger Mudd reported that the organization, whose only concern had been about raising too much money, had gathered the grand sum of $144.50. A comedian on a network program made fun of Scruggs. The audience got a good laugh out of it.

Scruggs wrote "Our memorial had to be paid for by private contributions in a largely volunteer effort organized by people whose principal reward would be knowing they had honored those whom the nation managed to ignore." The Vietnam Veterans Memorial Fund soon discovered that many people, for many different

Jan Scruggs was raised in Bowie, Maryland. After he graduated from high school he served with the U.S. Army's 199th Light Infantry Brigade. After valiantly serving his term in Vietnam he came home and attended American University in Washington, D.C., where he obtained a masters degree in counseling.

After spearheading creation of the Vietnam Veterans Memorial, Scruggs wrote his emotionally moving book, *To Heal a Nation*, which is a story based on the Vietnam War and the making of the memorial. In May 1988, the movie version was broadcast on NBC.

Recently, Scruggs wrote another book, *Why Vietnam Still Matters: the War and the Wall*, which is dedicated to high school students. Jan has appeared on *60 Minutes*, *Nightline*, and *Good Morning America*, and has served as host for the *Larry King Show*.

Scruggs currently is an independent businessman, attorney, and motivational speaker for some of the country's largest corporations. He also has spoken to the prestigious Million Dollar Roundtable with his simple yet highly powerful message: courage is life's great equalizer. He has thrilled hundreds of audiences over the last 10 years with his use of humor and quotations from some of America's great minds ranging from George Washington to Thomas Jefferson.

In the summer of 1980, five years after the last Americans left Vietnam, President Jimmy Carter signed a bill that granted two acres of land for a memorial to Vietnam veterans. The land was located on the National Mall, an open area between the U.S. Capitol and the White House, which also contains the Washington Monument, Lincoln Memorial, and Jefferson Memorial.

reasons, would take a personal stake in the success of this cause. A young girl who lost her father in the war sent $10. A vet with no job scraped together $5 and sent it to the committee. The parents of a young man who had been killed in the war sent a check for $25.

The fund-raising effort received a huge boost when Senator John Warner of Virginia donated $5,000 of his own money and helped raise another $50,000. Eventually, donations exceeded $8.4 million. The VVMF received private donations from more than 275,000 individuals.

Members of the VVMF decided that a site at the base of the Lincoln Memorial seemed perfect for their project. But the organization had to ask Congress for permission to build in that area of the National Mall. The wheels for site selection were set in motion when Jan Scruggs appeared before a Senate subcommittee with a briefcase full of documents justifying the site on the Mall.

The bill that granted the VVMF two acres at the foot of the Lincoln Memorial passed the Senate in just seven minutes on April 30, 1980. Two months later, on July 1, 1980, President Jimmy Carter signed the bill that allotted two acres of land, located under the gaze of Abraham Lincoln, to the Vietnam Veterans Memorial Fund (VVMF).

The veterans had their land. Now what? How could those who served in Vietnam be best honored?

Maya Ying Lin (center), an architecture student at Yale University, submitted the winning design for the Vietnam Veterans Memorial. With her in this May 6, 1981, photo are Jan Scruggs (left), the president of the VVMF, and Bob Doubek (right), a co-founder of the organization. Lin's design, which they are displaying in this picture, was one of nearly 1,500 submitted to the committee.

DESIGNING THE MEMORIAL

$\mathcal{T}$he VVMF decided a nationwide design competition, judged by a panel of architects and artists, would be the best way to find a design worthy of this challenge. Bob Doubek, a veteran and co-founder of the VVMF with Scruggs, stated the purpose of the design competition: "The hope is that the creation of the memorial will begin a healing process."

Designing a memorial that could somehow help people heal their emotional wounds must have seemed quite a difficult task to those who submitted entries. Imagine the challenge of creating something that would not only honor the more than two million Americans who served in Vietnam, but that could also help the millions of family members and loved ones of the more than 58,200 dead and missing soldiers begin to heal. Could this even be done?

More than 1,000 people attempted to find a way. Those who submitted entries were given four criteria to follow in their designs: the design had to be reflective and *contemplative*, it had to be *harmonious* with the site, it had to be inscribed with the names of the dead and missing, and it could not contain any political statement about war.

With only those *directives* to guide them, 1,421 individuals submitted entries. After four days of closed-door deliberations, entry number 1,026 was the unanimous choice. Many were surprised to discover that the winner was a 21-year-old Chinese-American woman named Maya Ying Lin, an undergraduate college student at Yale.

At the time Lin was instructed to enter the VVMF design competition as a requirement for an architecture course. She had never experienced the death of someone close to her. Lin wondered how she would create a design that could help an entire nation begin a healing process. She visited the future site of the memorial on the National Mall to help visualize her design.

"I thought about what death is, what a loss is," remembered Lin. "A sharp pain that lessens with time, but can never quite heal over. The idea occurred to me there on the site. I had an impulse to cut open the earth. The grass would grow back, but the cut would remain."

Back at Yale, it took Lin only three weeks to complete her design.

Maya Ying Lin's design consisted of a long, black granite wall upon which the names of the men and women who had died in the war or were missing in action would be etched. It sought to honor their collective sacrifice.

Initially, however, the design was not well received. A veteran assailed the design as the "black gash of shame."

Maya Ying Lin was born in 1959 in Athens, Ohio. An architect and sculptor, she comes from an artistically distinguished Chinese family that immigrated to the United States in the 1940s.

Lin attended the Yale University School of Architecture and graduated in 1981 with a bachelor's degree and in 1986 with a master's degree.

After designing the Vietnam Veterans Memorial, Lin cemented her status as a major figure of modern architecture with her sculptural design for the Civil Rights Memorial in Montgomery, Alabama in 1989 and a monument commemorating coeducation at Yale University in 1991. More recently, she has also executed other kinds of architectural projects including several private houses, the Museum of African Art, and a huge clock at Pennsylvania Station in New York City. Lin has also designed furniture and created sculptures.

Whatever the context or scale of the work, Lin is known for her visual poetry and sensitive mingling of highly abstract form with meaning.

President Ronald Reagan holds a model of the Three Servicemen sculpture at the Vietnam Veterans Memorial. Jan Scruggs, the Vietnam veteran who was a driving force behind the memorial, is at the left.

Other detractors criticized it as a "black, flagless pit," while others attacked it as being "unheroic," "death-oriented," and "intentionally not meaningful."

Supporters of her design felt that personal, political, or ethical reservations about the war could be set aside in order to remember and honor those who served. The memorial could begin the healing and *reconciliation* process of a still-divided nation. But before the nation could heal, old wounds needed to be opened.

The veterans were not new to wounds; they had suffered many. Serving in America's most divisive war since the Civil War, they fought in a foreign country against *guerrilla* tactics and an enemy that included women and children. Indecision and protests at home during the war gave way to indifference and hostility against the veterans upon their return. As they fought to make a life for themselves after the war, the veterans' shared experiences provided a common bond. Now, for the first time, they were divided, poised to inflict possible injury to that bond.

As debate raged over Maya Ying Lin's design, opponents suggested throwing it out and starting over again. Members of Congress registered their disapproval. James Watt, secretary of the interior in the Reagan administration, refused to issue a building permit for the memorial. Under the threat of losing their memorial, the veterans, their supporters, and their opponents met to find a compromise. They decided to add a statue and a flagpole. These would symbolize in a more tradi-

> **The granite used for the memorial comes from Bangalore, India; it was cut and fabricated at Barre, Vermont.**

tional manner the patriotism and heroism that some thought was lacking in Lin's design.

In the end, the compromise of the Three Servicemen statue and flagpole fulfilled a purpose of the Vietnam Veterans Memorial–to help heal the nation's wounds. Citing pain as "a necessary part of ... the healing process for the wounds of Vietnam," a former design opponent, Milt Copulos, confessed that although "the wall of the memorial could have been a wall between us," it instead "became a bridge."

A visitor to the Vietnam Veterans Memorial touches the name of a family member who died during the war. The Vietnam Veterans Memorial continues to be, as the design jury noted, "a place of quiet reflection, and a tribute to those who served their nation in difficult times. All who come here can find it a place of healing."

A GROWING TRIBUTE

Since its dedication on Veterans Day in 1982, millions have visited the wall. Some come and make rubbings of names; some leave special mementos at the memorial, some simply touch the black granite and whisper a name.

But perhaps most important is what the memorial has come to mean. The wall is simple, thoughtful, and profound. It is a place to remember those who served during a turbulent time in American history. It is also a place for the nation to heal its wounds.

The Vietnam Veterans Memorial wall contains the names of more than 58,200 men and women who were killed or remain missing from that war. The names are etched on black granite panels that compose the wall. The panels are arranged into two arms, extending from a central point to form a wide angle. Each arm points to either the Washington Monument or the Lincoln Memorial to bring the memorial into a historical context on the National Mall.

The wall is built into the earth, below ground level. The area within the wall's angle has been contoured to form a gentle sloped approach toward the center of the wall. While entering the memorial at ground level from either end of its arms, the descent to the center reveals more and more of the wall until it towers more that ten feet above the walkway. The center—within the protection of the arms of the memorial and surrounded by the grassy slope—is a place of quiet calmness and serenity.

On the granite wall itself, the layout of the names perhaps most strongly conveys the significance of the memorial. The names are listed *chronologically*, according to the date the servicemen and women

The Department of Defense determines which names are placed on the wall according to criteria specified in Presidential Executive Orders from Presidents Johnson and Nixon. Those orders specified Vietnam and adjacent coastal waters, and later Laos and Cambodia, as a combat zone. Those who have died as a result of Agent Orange-related diseases or post-traumatic stress suicides are not included on the wall.

Each year thousands of people visit the Vietnam Veterans Memorial. Many come to find the names of friends or loved ones who were killed during the Vietnam War; more than 58,200 names are carved into the black granite wall.

died or were declared missing. Thus the story of the Vietnam War, from beginning to end, is recorded on the wall. Finding a name would be like finding bodies on a battlefield, according to Lin.

The first name is located in the center of the memorial, at the top of the wall, under the date 1959, the year of the first death. The names continue line by line down each panel, as if each was a page in a book, towards the right end of the memorial. The names resume at the left end of the memorial and continue toward the center. It is here, at the bottom of the wall, where the last death is recorded, next to the date 1975.

As described by Lin, "The war's beginning and end meet; the war is 'complete,' coming full circle." By illustrating that the war has come to completion, perhaps the

Frederick E. Hart was a sculptor born in Atlanta, Georgia. He started out as a painter but was attracted to sculpture and decided he should learn the craft of stonecutting. In 1967 he got himself a job with the ongoing construction of the National Cathedral in Washington, D.C. Within a couple of years he was an apprentice stonecutter, rendering ornamental decorations.

In 1971, Hart opened his own studio to work out his ideas for the west façade of the cathedral, and in 1974 his design for the main entrance won an international competition. The finished work, carved from Indiana limestone in a traditional romantic-realist style, was dedicated in May 1990.

Before this, he had placed third in the competition for the Vietnam War Memorial; in the uproar that followed the choice of Maya Ying Lin's wall, he was awarded a second commission. His realistic bronze (pictured), known as *Three Servicemen* or *Three Fighting Men*, was dedicated in 1984. He later served on the board of the President's Commission on Fine Arts.

wall encourages visitors to move on to the next step of coping with their feelings about the war and those who served. In addition, the circular layout of the names may also suggest that the healing of the nation can also come full circle.

Other than the names, nothing on the wall describes who the men and women were. No name appears any more meaningful or important than any other. The names are distinguished only by how the men and women were lost. A diamond next to a name indicates a person was killed. A cross next to a name indicates a person is missing. More than 1,000 of the names on the wall are of people who remain missing.

The first additions to the wall occurred in 1983, the year after the memorial was dedicated. These 68 names were of Marines who were killed during the Vietnam War when their airplane crashed in Hong Kong. Fifteen more names were added in 1984. In 1986, 110 names were added when the geographic criteria were enlarged to include those who were part of the war effort but killed outside the war zone itself.

Since 1986, other additions have occurred when, through study and discovery, it was determined that names deserved to be placed on the wall. More often today, names added are of veterans who have recently died as a direct result of combat-related injuries received in the war. When the occasion arises, new names are etched into the wall around Memorial Day in the spring or Veterans Day in the fall. Since the names on the wall are listed chronologically according to casualty date and because space on the wall is limited, the new names are added as close as possible to the appropriate place where space allows.

Should a service member who is listed as missing-in-action on the wall ever return alive, a circle would be inscribed around the cross next to his name. To date, no such symbols are on the wall.

As concrete was being poured for the foundation of the Vietnam Veterans Memorial, a U.S. Navy officer walked up to the edge of the trench. He paused, threw something in, and saluted. It was his dead brother's Purple Heart. It was also the first offering left at the wall.

Who would have guessed that the Vietnam Veterans Memorial would become an altar of sorts—a place where people would leave offerings of love and remembrance? Who could have known that this Purple Heart would be the first of tens of thousands of items left at the wall? The park rangers and volunteers who worked at the wall knew only that the special objects had to be saved. This was the beginning of the Vietnam Veterans Memorial Collection.

This collection is unlike any museum collection anywhere. Among the artifacts are photographs, letters, MIA/POW bracelets, medals, helmets, dog tags, boots, canned food, unopened beer cans, cigarettes, birthday cards, toys, and bullets. Soldiers who returned home leave objects for those who did not. Many objects are from parents, spouses, siblings, and children. Some offerings are direct communications between the living and the dead; tangible bonds between those who were killed and those who remember. They tell us something about the people on the wall; but as well as any history book, they tell us about an era.

The Vietnam Veterans Memorial Collection was developed to preserve this special memorabilia. The collection is unique in that a museum curator chooses nothing. Those who lived through this turbulent time in American history choose many of these artifacts.

This American flag, decorated in memory of Marine Corps veterans, was draped over the fence at the Vietnam Veterans Memorial on Veterans Day 1992. Thousands of items have been left at the wall.

The walls of the memorial are 246.75 feet long and the angle where they come together is 125 degrees, 12 minutes. There are 140 pilings with the average depth to bedrock 35 feet. The height of the walls at the vertex is 10.1 feet.

Each day, park rangers collect the offerings, place them in individual bags, and tag them with the date, a description, and the number of the panel under which the offering was left. They are then transferred to a large storage facility about 12 miles from the wall. There, the items are carefully organized and preserved. The artifacts are so socially and historically significant that the Smithsonian Museum of American History has a large sample of the collection on display. Through these highly personal messages from the living to the dead, visitors will be able to see, for centuries to come, the impact of the Vietnam War on this country.

Why do people leave these offerings? The reasons behind them are as varied as the items themselves. Men pay off old debts, leaving dollars, cigarettes, and cans of beer. A woman left two sonograms for the grandfather her children would never know. A park ranger tells the story of another woman who left her wedding ring at the wall. She was getting remarried the next day and wanted to say goodbye to, and let go of, her first husband, who had died in Vietnam.

Perhaps the letters and cards say the most. Their words portray feelings of rage, despair, loneliness, loss, and guilt. People leave cards for birthdays, Father's Day, and other holidays. But by communicating with loved ones through the wall, people are able to confront feelings they may have *repressed* for years. They can make peace with themselves and others as pain and guilt are released.

Over the years, the letters are increasingly revealing love, forgiveness, and hope. In this way, the Vietnam Veterans Memorial is much more than a way to honor those men and women who served their country. It has become a way for a whole nation to heal.

Today, the VVMF collaborates with the National Park Service to conduct ceremonies at the memorial on Memorial Day and Veterans Day, to add those names of military personnel who are determined to have died as a result of their service in Southeast Asia during the Vietnam War, to keep records of those listed on the wall, and to maintain residual funds for the maintenance and repair of the memorial.

In 1984, former Army nurse and Vietnam veteran Diane Carlson Evans founded the Vietnam Women's Memorial Project to honor the more than 265,000 women who served during the war, including 10,000 in Vietnam. After a nine-year

> Since the Vietnam Veterans Memorial was dedicated, names have been added to the wall and changes made to the existing names. Originally the wall contained 57,939 names. The wall today has more than 58,200 names.

struggle, a monument to the women who served in Vietnam was constructed. just a few hundred yards away from the wall. The women's memorial features a sculpture by Glenna Goodacre that shows three Vietnam-era women in battle dress. While one nurse cares for a wounded soldier, another kneels in thought or prayer. The third looks to the skies–for help from a helicopter or, perhaps, from a higher power. Goodacre

Glenna Goodacre was born in Texas and began her art career there. She graduated from Colorado College and studied at the Art Students League in New York.

Since the Vietnam Women's Memorial was installed on the National Mall in 1993, the bronze sculpture has been seen by millions of visitors to Washington and has been filmed and photographed extensively by the media.

Before creating the women's memorial, however, Goodacre enjoyed a successful 20-year career as an artist. Known for her portrait busts and figures and for her interesting sculptural compositions of active children, Goodacre also had a successful career as a painter.

Goodacre has more than 40 bronze portraits in public collections in the United States, including sculptures of Dwight D. Eisenhower, Barbara Jordan, Katherine Anne Porter, Lt. Karl W. Richter, Dr. Norris Bradbury, Greer Garson, and Gen. Harry H. "Hap" Arnold. She also has created a seven-foot standing portrait of former President Ronald Reagan for the National Cowboy Hall of Fame and designed the golden dollar coin depicting Shoshoni guide Sacagawea and her infant son.

Goodacre divides her time between Santa Fe, New Mexico, where she has maintained a studio since 1983, and Dallas, Texas, where her husband has a law practice.

Diane Carlson Evans holds the hand of a bronze soldier as sculptor Glenna Goodacre looks on at the Vietnam Women's Memorial.

left the interpretation open so that people could read into it whatever they wish. The bronze sculpture is almost seven feet tall and weighs 2,000 pounds.

Support for the women's memorial came from all over. Letters pored in from both male and female veterans. Nurses spoke of the horrors of war. Veterans remembered the nurses with love and affection–the kind smile, the gentle touch, and the soft words that eased their pain. Without the nurses, Evans felt, the Vietnam Veterans Memorial wall would have stretched for 50 miles.

In November 1993, the Vietnam Women's Memorial was dedicated, just a few hundred feet from the wall.

1945 Ho Chi Minh reads Vietnam's Declaration of Independence and establishes the Democratic Republic of Vietnam in Hanoi on September 2.

1946 The French army returns to Vietnam; Ho Chi Minh establishes the Viet Minh, a guerrilla army; on December 19, the war against the French begins.

1950 The U.S. begins to help support the French in Vietnam.

1955 The U.S. backed Ngo Dinh Diem government organizes the Republic of Vietnam as an independent nation; Diem declares himself president.

1959 The first American combat death in Vietnam occurs on July 8.

1960 The National Liberation Front, also called the Viet Cong, is founded in South Vietnam.

1961 The U.S. military buildup in Vietnam begins.

1963 South Vietnamese President Diem is assassinated on November 1.

1964 A trade embargo is imposed on North Vietnam on May 4 in response to attacks on South Vietnam; in early August, President Lyndon Johnson asks Congress for a resolution against North Vietnam following the Gulf of Tonkin incident; on August 5, Congress approves the Gulf of Tonkin Resolution, which allows the president to take any necessary measures to repel further attacks and to provide military assistance to any member of the Southeast Asia Treaty Organization.

1965 Generals Ky and Thieu seize control of the South Vietnamese government in June.

1967 Thieu is elected president of South Vietnam in September; 50,000 people demonstrate against the war in Washington, D.C. from October 21–23.

1969 The Paris peace talks begin on May 20; on July 8, President Richard Nixon announces the first troop withdrawals from South Vietnam; Ho Chi Minh dies on September 2;

more than 250,000 people gather for anti-war protest held in Washington, D.C. on November 15.

1970 The armies of the U.S. and South Vietnam invade Cambodia on April 30; four students protesting the war are killed by National Guardsmen at Kent State University in Ohio on May 4; more than 100 colleges are closed on May 6 due to student riots over what happened at Kent State.

1973 The U.S. and North Vietnam sign Paris cease-fire agreements on January 23, ending the American combat role in war; U.S. military draft ends; in February, U.S. prisoners of war begin coming home.

1975 North Vietnam forces take over Saigon on April 30; South Vietnam surrenders to North Vietnam, ending the war and reunifying the country under Communist control.

1979 Veteran Jan Scruggs conceives idea for memorial to honor those who served in Vietnam.

1980 On April 30, Congress votes in favor of giving Vietnam Veterans Memorial Funds two acres of land near the Lincoln Memorial; President Jimmy Carter signs bill giving VVMF the land on July 1.

1981 Maya Ling Yin's design is selected from 1,421 entries to be constructed as the Vietnam Veterans Memorial.

1982 Construction of memorial begins in March; it is dedicated on November 13.

1984 Diane Carlson Evans starts the Vietnam Women's Memorial Project.

1986 Fundraising for the VWMP begins.

1988 President Ronald Reagan signs bill in November to authorize women's memorial.

1991 Glenna Goodacre selected to design women's memorial.

1993 Women's memorial dedicated in November.

2001 More than 4.4 million people visit the Vietnam Wall.

chronologically—telling a story in the order of events from the earliest to the latest.

Communism—a form of government under which the state owns everything.

corrupt—characterized by improper conduct.

contemplative—to look at something thoughtfully.

directive—an authoritative order.

etched—to produce an image on a hard surface such as glass or stone.

guerrilla—a military strategy of using surprise raids to harass the enemy.

harmonious—agreement in feeling or action.

infantryman—soldier who fights on foot with rifles, hand grenades and machine guns.

oppressive—unjustly harsh and mean.

rebels—people who rises up against the government.

reconciliation—to cease hostility or opposition.

repressed—kept under control.

scrutinized—looked at carefully.

subside—to sink to a low or lower level.

symbolism—something used to represent something else.

tangible—something that is real and can be touched.

weathered—showing signs of life in a harsh environment.

FURTHER READING

Becker, Elizabeth. *America's Vietnam War: A Narrative History*. New York: Clarion, 1992.

Hass, Kristen Ann. *Carried to the Wall*. Los Angeles: University of California Press, 1998.

Meyer, Peter. *The Wall: A Day at the Vietnam Veterans Memorial*. New York: Thomas Dunne Books, 1993.

Morrissey, Thomas F. *Between the Lines: Photographs from the National Vietnam Veterans Memorial*. Syracuse, N.Y.: Syracuse University Press, 2000.

Scruggs, Jan, and Joel L. Swerdlow. *To Heal a Nation*. New York: Harper and Row, 1985

INTERNET RESOURCES

The National Park Service: Vietnam Veterans Memorial
http://www.nps.gov/vive/home

Information on the Vietnam Wall
http://www.thewall-usa.com
http://www.themovingwall.org
http://www.vietvet.org/thewall.htm

PICTURE CREDITS

BARRY MORENO has been librarian and historian at the Ellis Island Immigration Museum and the Statue of Liberty National Monument since 1988. He is the author of *The Statue of Liberty Encyclopedia*, which was published by Simon and Schuster in October 2000. He is a native of Los Angeles, California. After graduation from California State University at Los Angeles, where he earned a degree in history, he joined the National Park Service as a seasonal park ranger at the Statue of Liberty; he eventually became the monument's librarian. In his spare time, Barry enjoys reading, writing, and studying foreign languages and grammar. His biography has been included in *Who's Who Among Hispanic Americans*, *The Directory of National Park Service Historians*, *Who's Who in America*, and *The Directory of American Scholars*.

JOSEPH FERRY is a veteran journalist who has written for several newspapers in Philadelphia and the surrounding suburbs. He lives in Sellersville, Pennsylvania, with his wife and three children. His other books in Mason Crest's AMERICAN SYMBOLS AND THEIR MEANINGS series are *The Jefferson Memorial, The National Anthem,* and *The American Flag.*